CAPTAIN SCOTT

Written and illustrated by Nigel Baines

Collins

This picture shows a group of explorers after they finally reached the South Pole. Their journey there was one of extreme hardship in one of the least-explored and most **inhospitable** landmasses on Earth.

Even so, they don't look happy at having reached the Pole do they? Why? Because this is the group led by Captain Scott. The year is 1912. After a near two-year **expedition** and an 880-mile (1,416-kilometre) trek to become the first men to reach the South Pole, they arrive to find they have been beaten by the Norwegian explorer, Roald Amundsen.

They are dispirited, running low on food and now have an 880-mile return journey. With a rare weather event that occurs only every 15 years ahead of them, their troubles have barely begun ...

Robert Falcon Scott was born in England in 1868 at a time when Great Britain's empire extended to over a fifth of the world. It was a time of confidence and great scientific advances. However, when we look back, it is clear that the British Empire was extremely **hostile** to other cultures, and regularly **exploited** them to gain **profit** and **territory**.

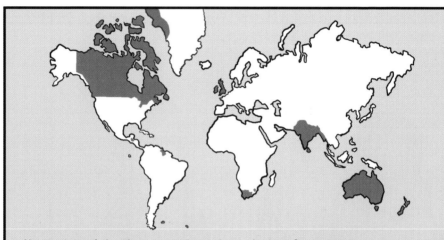

Having joined the Navy at 13, Scott showed a lot of promise. As a teenager, he was spotted as a possible leader for an Antarctic expedition.

He's a fine boy and I have an idea he could be the future captain we've been looking for.

Back home, Scott was married to the sculptor Kathleen Bruce, and they had a son, Peter. Scott was close friends with J.M. Barrie who wrote the stories featuring Peter Pan after whom Scott named his son. Scott loved writing and had always wanted to be a writer, while Barrie had always wanted to be an explorer!

Oh, how I long to write as beautifully as you, James.

Ha! It seems we would each feel much happier living each other's lives!

Scott had already led a three-year expedition to Antarctica from 1901–1904. During that time, he had endured many trials but never reached the South Pole. Scott's first expedition was for scientific purposes but the dream of being the first to reach the Pole was firmly planted in his mind.

Scott spent 18 months planning every detail for his second expedition.

How much food do we need? How long will it take? How much will it cost?!!

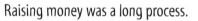
Raising money was a long process.

We need every single penny we can get.

There was no shortage of volunteers for crew members, with over 8,000 applying!

Scott eventually chose his crew of 65 men.

Now I just need a ship!

Scott wanted to buy his old ship, but this wasn't allowed, so he chose the *Terra Nova*, an old whaling ship. To ensure the ship could sail through thick ice, it was reinforced with two metres of oak. On 15th June 1910, the expedition set off, sailing first to Cape Town and then to Melbourne.

Meanwhile, a Norwegian explorer, Roald Amundsen, had been exploring an area called the Northwest Passage and intended to go on to the North Pole. When he found out that another ship had just reached there, he changed his plans. But he kept this a secret, telling only his brother as he turned his ship towards the South Pole.

We must go south but if I tell this news now, word will get out. We need to get a head start on the *Terra Nova*.

As he wasn't going for scientific purposes, Amundsen could focus on getting there quickly. He sent Scott a **telegram** from his ship: "Beg leave to inform you proceeding Antarctic."

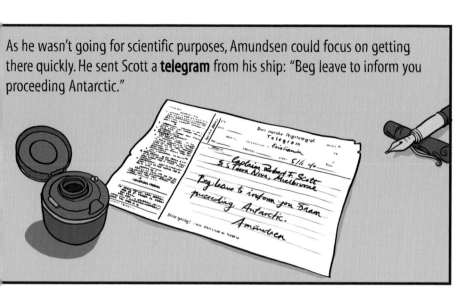

Amundsen was nearly **bankrupt** and knew that a spectacular expedition could save him financially. Attitudes were very different at that time though, and Amundsen's decision was seen as unsporting behaviour. This forever haunted him.

Equipment

The Norwegians were experienced skiers. They took a full complement of husky dogs and were expert dog handlers. Amundsen's men also had **Inuit furs** which they wore loose to stop sweat on their skin from freezing, which can be very dangerous.

Scott's party took a lot of scientific equipment and their own self-assembly hut! They took 33 dogs (Amundsen took 100) but also ponies and three mechanical vehicles, one of which was lost in the ice when unloading the ship.

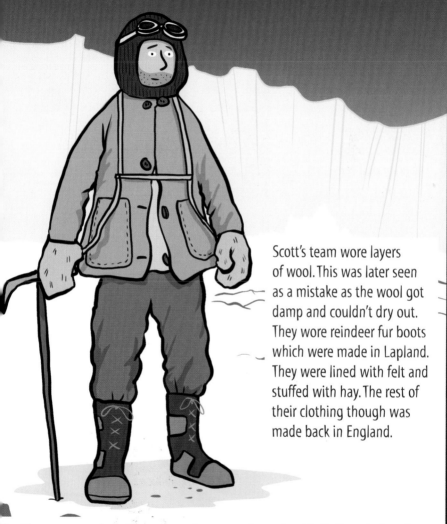

Scott's team wore layers of wool. This was later seen as a mistake as the wool got damp and couldn't dry out. They wore reindeer fur boots which were made in Lapland. They were lined with felt and stuffed with hay. The rest of their clothing though was made back in England.

Scott's men were also reluctant to rely too much on the skis. Pulling sledges by hand was considered a more noble activity. Some of the preparations now seem a little foolish: Scott's team took 35,000 cigars!

After sailing to New Zealand, the *Terra Nova* was heavily loaded with all the supplies (including the self-assembly hut!) and left for Antarctica on 29th November 1910. Remember, this is the **southern hemisphere** where it is summer in November and the best time to travel. However, just two days into the journey, they hit a terrible storm.

the route south

Due to being overloaded, the *Terra Nova* only narrowly escaped **capsizing** in the rough seas. Some ponies were washed overboard and others became very ill in the wretched conditions. As awful as it was, the old ship bore the storm well.

She seems like a living thing fighting a great fight!

At one point, Osman, Scott's favourite Siberian husky dog, washed overboard and was washed back by the next wave!

After surviving the crossing, they finally reached the great continent, but it still took three weeks for the ship to break through all the **pack ice** that protected it.

It's almost as though the land doesn't want her secrets to be given up.

In January 1911, the explorers finally landed and erected their hut at Cape Evans. The hut was very large and had everything they needed for a base – it is still there today. What an adventure they'd had already! They'd been travelling for seven months and must have been tired but had yet to start their main objective.

It's hard to believe we are so far from home. It feels so warm and homely here.

They now had to wait and let the coming winter pass before attempting the journey to the Pole later in the year. They played football when possible.

Lectures were organised and they even produced their own newspaper, the *South Polar Times*, which had puzzles, poems, articles, cartoons and watercolour Illustrations!

You should feel very proud. It's the best-read newspaper on the continent!

In June and July, three members of the party, Wilson, Cherry and Bowers, undertook a perilous journey of 70 miles (113 kilometres) to collect and study emperor penguin eggs.

I can't think of a better way of having a bad time

I do not believe anybody on Earth has a worse time than an emperor penguin.

When they returned, they discovered that their tent had been destroyed so they had to construct a makeshift igloo from snow and rocks – in –40 degrees! The cold was so fierce that Cherry lost most of his teeth when they shattered because they were chattering so violently. That one journey alone has now become a famous book called *The Worst Journey in the World*.

While all this went on, Scott and a few men trekked into the continent, laying supply **depots** to prepare for their journey to the Pole. The vehicles they used often broke down and the ponies were not suited to the conditions. As a result, a depot they called One Ton Depot was laid 37 miles (60 kilometres) short of where they had intended. This would prove to be disastrous.

Finally, on 1st November 1911, Scott and his team set out for the South Pole. The group included ponies, dogs and two motorised sledges.

Well, men, let the march begin!

It's −22 degrees but it feels so hot! The sun's glare is intense.

Hmmm ... we must be careful. If we sweat too much, our clothes will get wet and never dry.

Before long, the journey became too much for the ponies, who often sank into the snow. Scott was very concerned for their welfare and eventually, the ten ponies that had survived the sea storm **perished**.

The land was brutal and unforgiving, but spectacular.

They crossed the Ross Ice Shelf and then, just before the Beardmore Glacier crossing, they faced another problem.

The dogs are running low on food.

We have no choice but to send them back to Camp Evans.

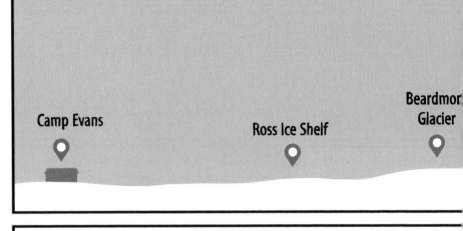

Camp Evans

Ross Ice Shelf

Beardmor
Glacier

People often think Antarctica is flat but it is very mountainous. It is technically a desert, although it is the coldest one on Earth! The Pole sits on the Antarctic Plateau at nearly 3,000 metres. At this height, people can suffer from **altitude sickness** and **dehydration** – a further problem that Scott and his men faced.

I'm so thirsty and tired.

We'll camp now and use the **paraffin** to boil up some snow. It's vital that we all keep drinking.

Antarctic Plateau

The Pole

As they pushed on, the weather worsened and cruel, biting cold storms and blizzards attacked them from all sides.

4th January 1912 ...

It's time to send the support team back. But Bowers, I want you to carry on with me. Five of us will go to the Pole instead of four.

I can't believe it. I'll be going to the Pole!!

This was a **critical** decision. It meant that the support team had one less man to haul the equipment back and the team heading to the Pole had one more mouth to feed.

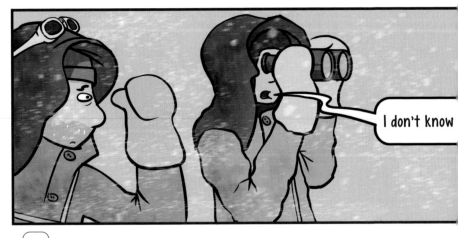

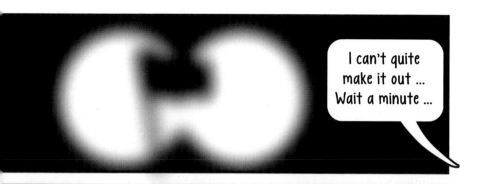

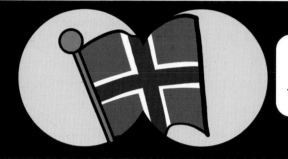

The next day, Scott and his team completed the punishing trek. It is hard to imagine the devastation they must have felt at not arriving there first.

My men are dehydrated and exhausted, and frostbite and **scurvy** are taking hold.

Well, we have turned our back now on the goal of our ambition with sore feelings and must face 800 miles of solid dragging – and goodbye to most of the day-dreams!

And so, on 19th January 1912, Scott and his team began the terrible journey back, one painful step after another.

On 4th February, both Scott and Evans fell into a **crevasse**.

It was the second time Evans had fallen into one and he was already suffering from an infected cut on his hand.

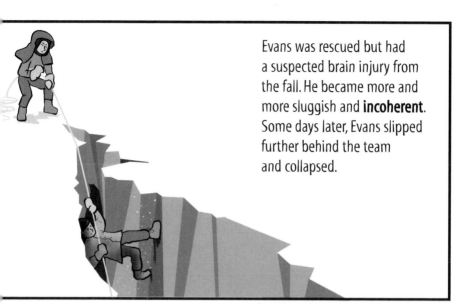

Evans was rescued but had a suspected brain injury from the fall. He became more and more sluggish and **incoherent**. Some days later, Evans slipped further behind the team and collapsed.

Don't worry, Evans, old chap. You won't have to suffer much more.

EVANS!!

The weather worsened dramatically on 27th February and **frostbite** started to affect the men.

I'm worried about Oates' feet.

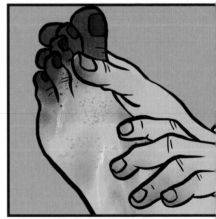

What is it, Bowers?

We're losing paraffin, sir, and I don't know why. But it means we'll have to **ration** it and not use the stoves so much. And yet we need the stoves for food, water and heat.

They were losing paraffin due to "paraffin creep". In extreme cold, liquid paraffin slowly flows up and out of even a tightly screwed-on cap. Amundsen was aware of this and made sure that all of his team's cans were **soldered** shut.

The sudden drop in temperature meant ice crystals formed on the snow. This made the runners on the sledges less smooth. Suddenly, it was like dragging them through sand.

We can't keep up this pulling, that's certain.

It was the beginning of March. Confined to their tent, with few rations left, even small tasks, like putting on wet footwear in the morning took most of their energy. Scott knew they were doomed.

Poor Oates. He can't go on much longer.

The weather didn't break. Outside, a blizzard raged with a temperature of −40 degrees.

Oates, what are you doing?

I am just going outside and may be some time.

Oates walked out into the raging blizzard and was never seen again. Did he sacrifice himself to help the others survive?

We knew that poor Oates was walking to his death, but though we tried to dissuade him, we knew it was the act of a brave man and an English gentleman. We all hope to meet the end with a similar spirit, and assuredly the end is not far.

43

Scott, Bowers and Wilson remained. Bowers and Wilson had planned to try and go to the next depot but they never set off. They stayed in the tent for a further ten days, before Scott's last diary entry on 29th March. They were only 11 miles (19 kilometres) away from One Ton Depot which, had it been laid in the intended place, they would have already reached.

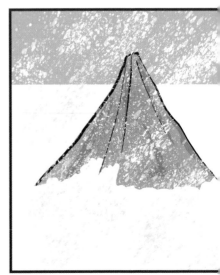

Every day we have been ready to start for our depot 11 miles away, but outside the door of our tent it remains a scene of whirling drift. I do not think we can hope for any better things now. We shall stick it out to the end, but we are getting weaker, of course, and the end cannot be far. It seems a pity, but I do not think I can write more.

R. Scott.

For God's sake look after our people.

A search party was eventually sent out and, on 12th November 1912, the tent and bodies of Scott and his team were found. Their papers and journals were collected but the bodies were simply wrapped in the tent and left.

In J.M. Barrie's book, Peter Pan says, "To die will be an awfully big adventure." That would not have been lost on Scott. It is quite fitting that the bodies of Scott and his team remain encased in the ice shelf to this day and that Antarctica is their Neverland.

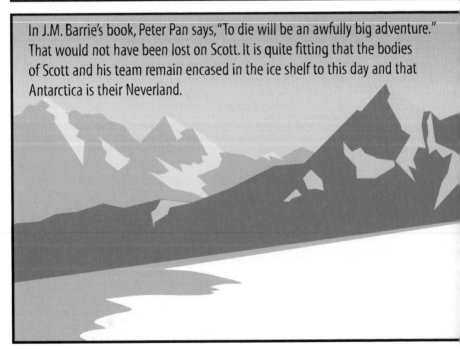

Back home in England, there was shock and sadness at the discovery but the myth of Captain Scott and his heroic efforts became established.

Scott's love of writing meant he kept excellent, descriptive written records of their journey.

He also had a professional photographer, Herbert Ponting, on his trip.

This, along with the classic English love of the heroic failure at the time, turned Scott into an instant hero. Statues were erected to **commemorate** him.

Amundsen didn't keep written records so well and photographs of his journey were poor. Somehow, despite his achievement, he was looked on in a lesser light and the first statue to commemorate him didn't go up until 1958! This statue of Scott is in Christchurch, New Zealand. Fittingly it was carved by his widow, Kathleen Scott.

Amundsen was criticised for turning the journey to the South Pole into a race. This had much to do with Victorian values of "fair play".

Amundsen was forever haunted by the death of Scott's party. In 1928, he was flying on a rescue mission in the Arctic when his plane disappeared. His body has never been found.

Was Scott a hero? In recent decades he has been criticised for poor decision-making and bad planning in some areas. However, there was no doubting his loyalty to his men – he wouldn't ask any of them to do something he couldn't do himself.

Glossary

altitude sickness sickness caused by climbing very high e.g. up a mountain

bankrupt People or companies that go bankrupt do not have enough money to pay their debts

capsizing a boat turning upside down

commemorate to remember an important person or event with a special ceremony or object

crevasse a large, deep crack in thick ice or rock

critical extremely important

dehydration loss of water from the body

depots places where large amounts of equipment or supplies are kept

devastating very shocking or upsetting

expedition an organised journey made for an exploration

exploited treated unfairly

frostbite a condition in which fingers or toes become seriously damaged as a result of being very cold

hostile unfriendly and aggressive

incoherent when someone is talking in a confused and unclear way

inhospitable unpleasant to live in

Inuit furs furs from the Inuit people, from Greenland or North America

paraffin a strong-smelling liquid which is used as a fuel in heaters, lamps and engines

perished died in harsh conditions

ration limiting the use of something to make it last

scurvy a disease that is caused by a lack of vitamin C

soldered when two pieces of metal are joined together by melting softer metal in the gap between them

southern hemisphere the half of Earth that lies south of the equator (the centre)

telegram a message that is sent electronically and then printed and delivered

Index

Scott's journey

Ideas for reading

Written by Gill Matthews
Primary Literacy Consultant

Reading objectives:
- read books that are structured in different ways and reading for a range of purposes
- draw inferences such as inferring characters' feelings, thoughts and motives from their actions, and justifying inferences with evidence
- identify how language, structure and presentation contribute to meaning
- retrieve, record and present information from non-fiction

Spoken language objectives:
- articulate and justify answers, arguments and opinions
- participate in discussions, presentations, performances, role play, improvisations and debates

Curriculum links: Geography – Locational knowledge, Geographical skills and fieldwork

Interest words: hardship, inhospitable, dispirited

Resources: IT; Maps and atlases

Build a context for reading

- Ask children to look at the front cover of the book and to read the title. Ask what they know about Captain Scott.
- Look at the back cover. Ask children to predict what they think the story might be about.
- Point out that this is a graphic novel. Check children's knowledge of the features of a graphic novel.
- Ask children to turn to the title page. Ask them what the fact that this is a statue of Captain Scott tells us about the man.

Understand and apply reading strategies

- Ask children to read pp2–11 and to summarise in writing what they have learnt about Captain Scott. Take feedback and discuss what they have found out.